D1212762

WATCH ANIMALS GROW

Kittens

by Colleen Sexton

BELLWETHER MEDIA • MINNEAPOLIS, MN

Note to Librarians, Teachers, and Parents:

Blastoff! Readers are carefully developed by literacy experts and combine standards-based content with developmentally appropriate text.

Level 1 provides the most support through repetition of high-frequency words, light text, predictable sentence patterns, and strong visual support.

Level 2 offers early readers a bit more challenge through varied simple sentences, increased text load, and less repetition of high-frequency words.

Level 3 advances early-fluent readers toward fluency through increased text and concept load, less reliance on visuals, longer sentences, and more literary language.

Level 4 builds reading stamina by providing more text per page, increased use of punctuation, greater variation in sentence patterns, and increasingly challenging vocabulary.

Level 5 encourages children to move from "learning to read" to "reading to learn" by providing even more text, varied writing styles, and less familiar topics.

Whichever book is right for your reader, Blastoff! Readers are the perfect books to build confidence and encourage a love of reading that will last a lifetime!

This edition first published in 2008 by Bellwether Media.

Library of Congress Cataloging-in-Publication Data
Sexton, Colleen A., 1967-
Kittens / by Colleen Sexton.
p. cm. – (Blastoff! readers: watch animals grow)
Summary: "A basic introduction to kittens. Simple text and full color photographs. Developed by literacy experts for students in kindergarten through third grade"–Provided by publisher.
Includes bibliographical references and index.
ISBN-13: 978-1-60014-168-3 (hardcover : alk. paper)
ISBN-10: 1-60014-168-4 (hardcover : alk. paper)
1. Kittens–Juvenile literature. I. Title.

SF445.7.S49 2008
636.8'07–dc22 2007040273

Newborn Kittens 4
What Kittens Eat 8
What Kittens Do 14
Kittens Snuggle 20
Glossary 22
To Learn More 23
Index 24

A mother cat gives birth to kittens. They are tiny and weak. Their eyes are closed.

Kittens sleep next
to their mother.
Their mother
keeps them warm.

Kittens drink
milk from
their mother.
It makes them
grow fast.

Soon they open their eyes. They walk on weak legs. They grow **whiskers**.

Kittens get their baby teeth.
Now they can eat **kitten food**.

Kittens have soft fur. They lick their fur to keep it clean.

Kittens play.
They chase toys.
They use their
sharp **claws**
to climb.

Soon kittens learn to leap. They can jump far and land on all four feet.

Purrr. This kitten likes to snuggle.

Glossary

claws—sharp, curved nails at the end of an animal's toes

kitten food—food for kittens; kitten food is made from meat, grains, and vegetables.

whiskers—thick, strong hairs on an animal's face used to feel things

To Learn More

AT THE LIBRARY

Dolbear, Emily J. *Cats Have Kittens.* Minneapolis, Minn.: Compass Point Books, 2001.

Meyers, Susan. *Kittens! Kittens! Kittens!* New York: Abrams Books for Young Readers, 2007.

Simon, Seymour. *Cats.* New York: HarperCollins, 2004.

ON THE WEB

Learning more about kittens is as easy as 1, 2, 3.

1. Go to www.factsurfer.com
2. Enter "kittens" into search box.
3. Click the "Surf" button and you will see a list of related web sites.

With factsurfer.com, finding more information is just a click away.

Index

claws, 16
eyes, 4, 10
feet, 18
fur, 14
kitten food, 12
legs, 10
milk, 8
mother, 4, 6, 8
teeth, 12
toys, 16
whiskers, 10

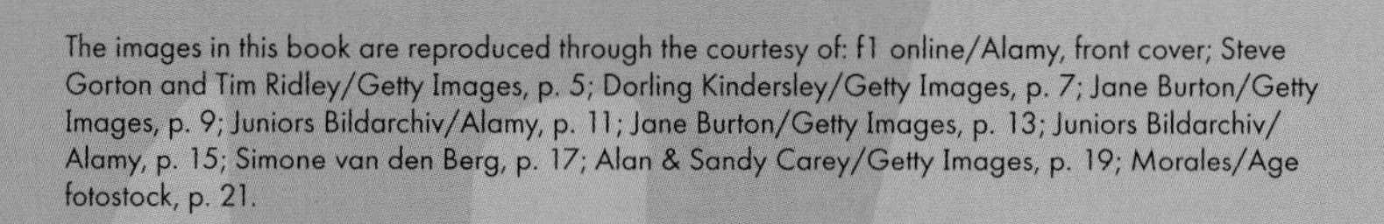

The images in this book are reproduced through the courtesy of: f1 online/Alamy, front cover; Steve Gorton and Tim Ridley/Getty Images, p. 5; Dorling Kindersley/Getty Images, p. 7; Jane Burton/Getty Images, p. 9; Juniors Bildarchiv/Alamy, p. 11; Jane Burton/Getty Images, p. 13; Juniors Bildarchiv/Alamy, p. 15; Simone van den Berg, p. 17; Alan & Sandy Carey/Getty Images, p. 19; Morales/Age fotostock, p. 21.